THE ENGLISH GRADUAL

PART II — THE PROPER

SUPPLEMENT

THE ENGLISH GRADUAL

PART II
SUPPLEMENT

Edited by
ARTHUR W. CLARKE
Musical Director of the Gregorian Association

Published by the
PLAINCHANT PUBLICATIONS COMMITTEE
6 HYDE PARK GATE, LONDON, S.W.7

THE CONCEPTION OF THE B.V. MARY

750

Introit　　　　　　　　　　　　　　　　　　　　　Tone VII

Cantors: I will greatly rejoice in the Lord my God; yea, my soul shall be joyful and glad in him; for he hath clothed me with the garments of *Choir:* sal-va-tion: he hath covered me with the robe of righteousness, as a bride adorneth her-self with her jew-els. *FINE*

Ps. I will magnify Thee, O Lord, for thou hast set me up: *Choir* and not made my foes to tri-umph ov-er me. *Cantors* Glo-ry be to the Father, and to the Son, and to the *Choir* Ho-ly Ghost. As it was in the beginning, is now, and ev-er shall be: world with-out end. A-men. *Full* I will *(etc.)*

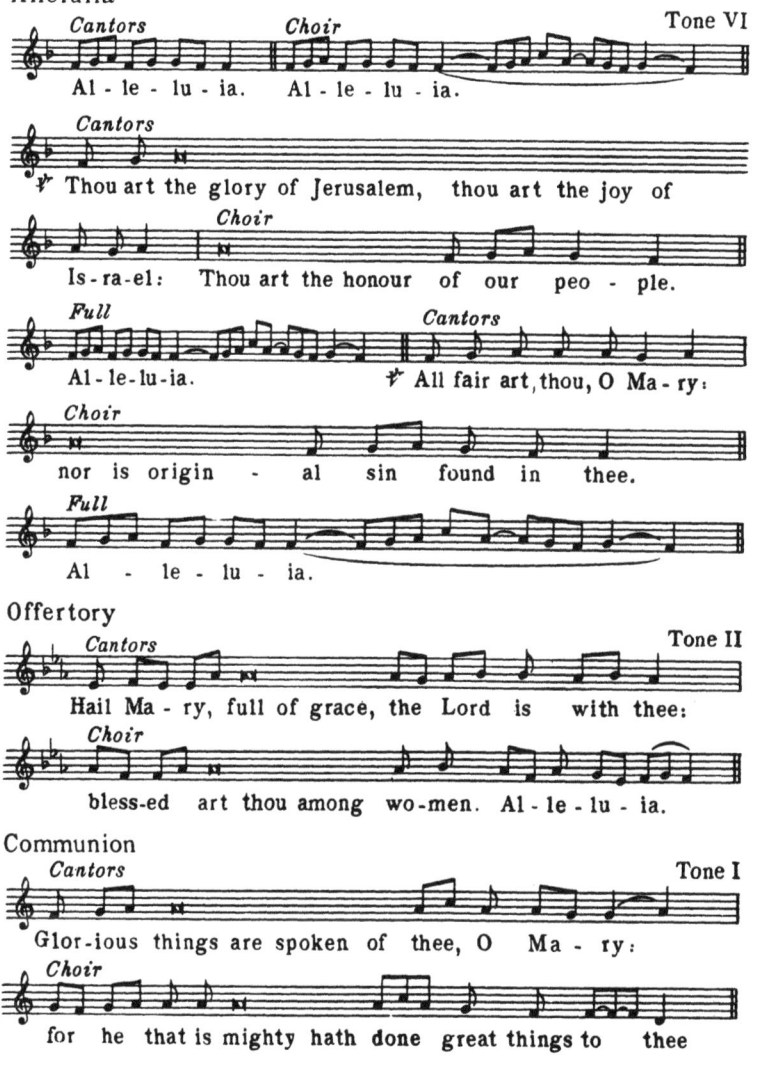

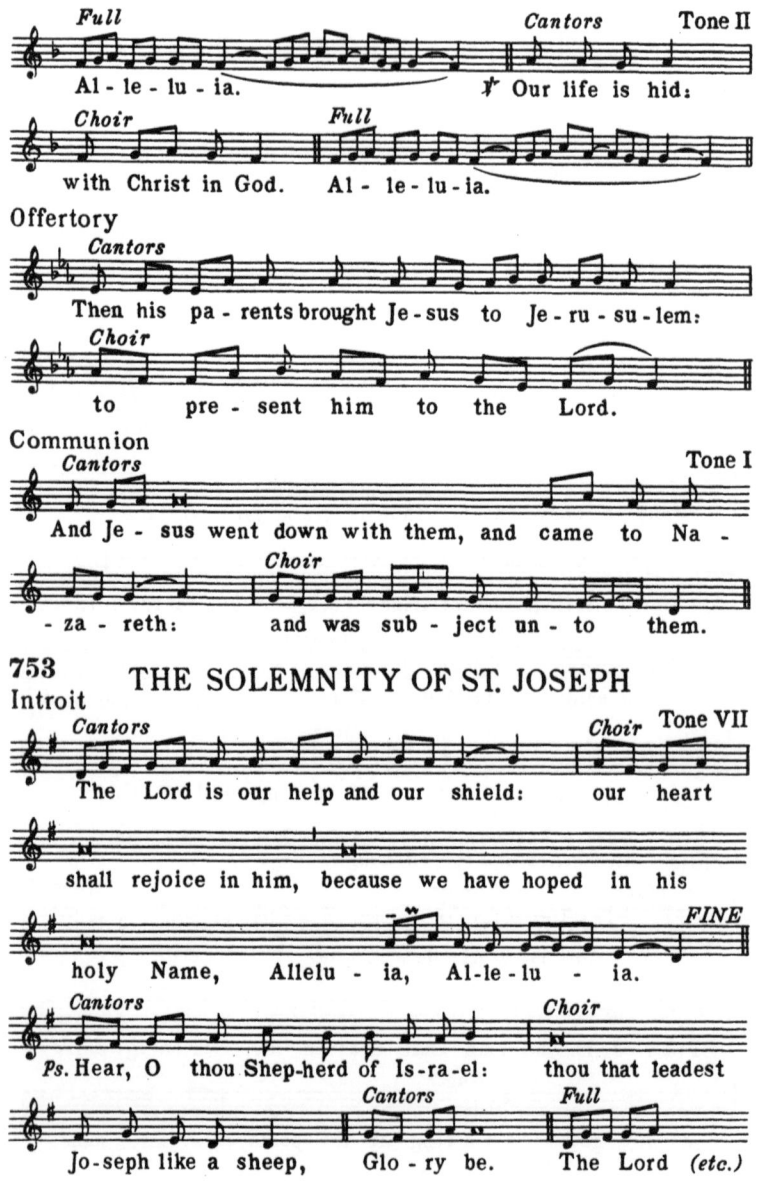

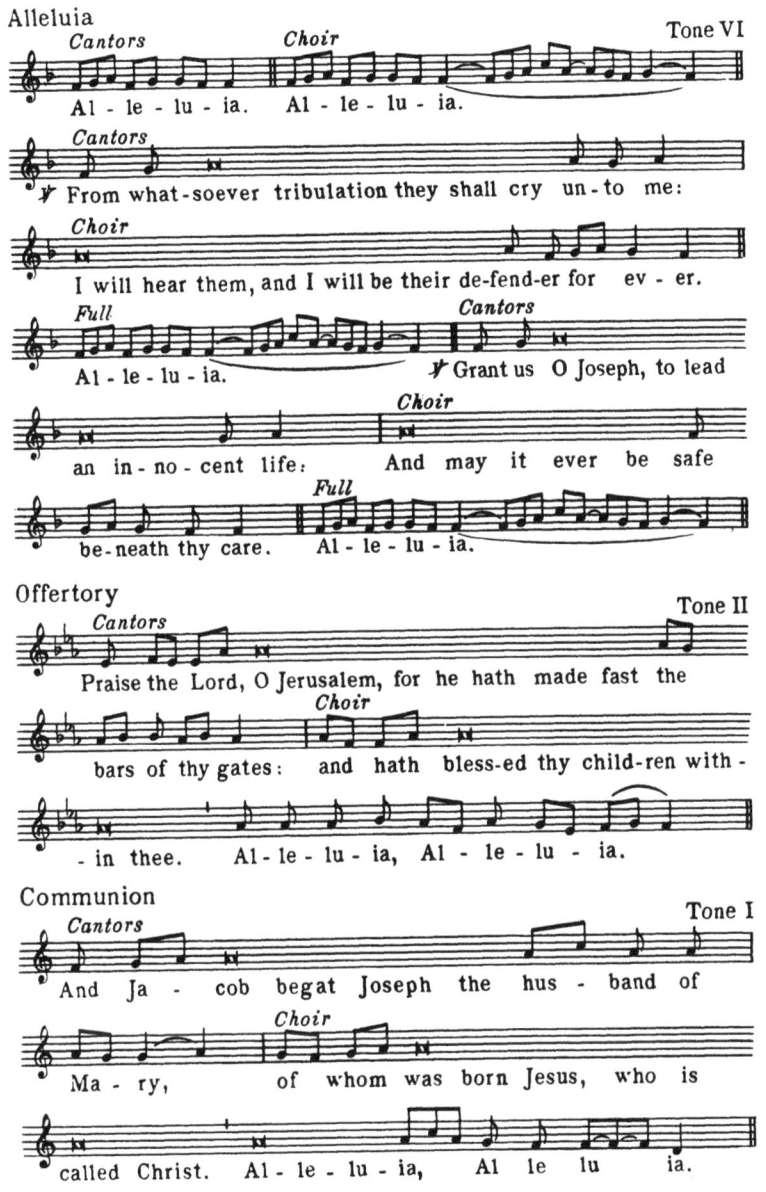

754 ST. AUGUSTINE OF CANTERBURY

Introit — Tone VII

Cantors: Let thy priests, O Lord, be clothed with righteousness; and let thy Saints sing with joy-ful-ness:

Choir: for thy servant David's sake, turn not away the presence of thine a-noint-ed. *FINE*

During Eastertide

For thy servant Davids sake, turn not away the presence of thine anointed. Allelu-ia. Al-le-lu-ia.

Cantors: Ps. Lord re-mem-ber Da-vid: *Choir:* and all his trou-ble.

Cantors: Glo-ry be: *Full:* Let thy priests *(etc.)*

Gradual — Tone V

Cantors: I will deck her priests with health: *Choir:* and her saints shall re-joice and sing. ℣ *Cantors:* There shall I make the horn of David to flour-ish *Choir:* I have ordained a lan-tern for mine a-noint-ed.

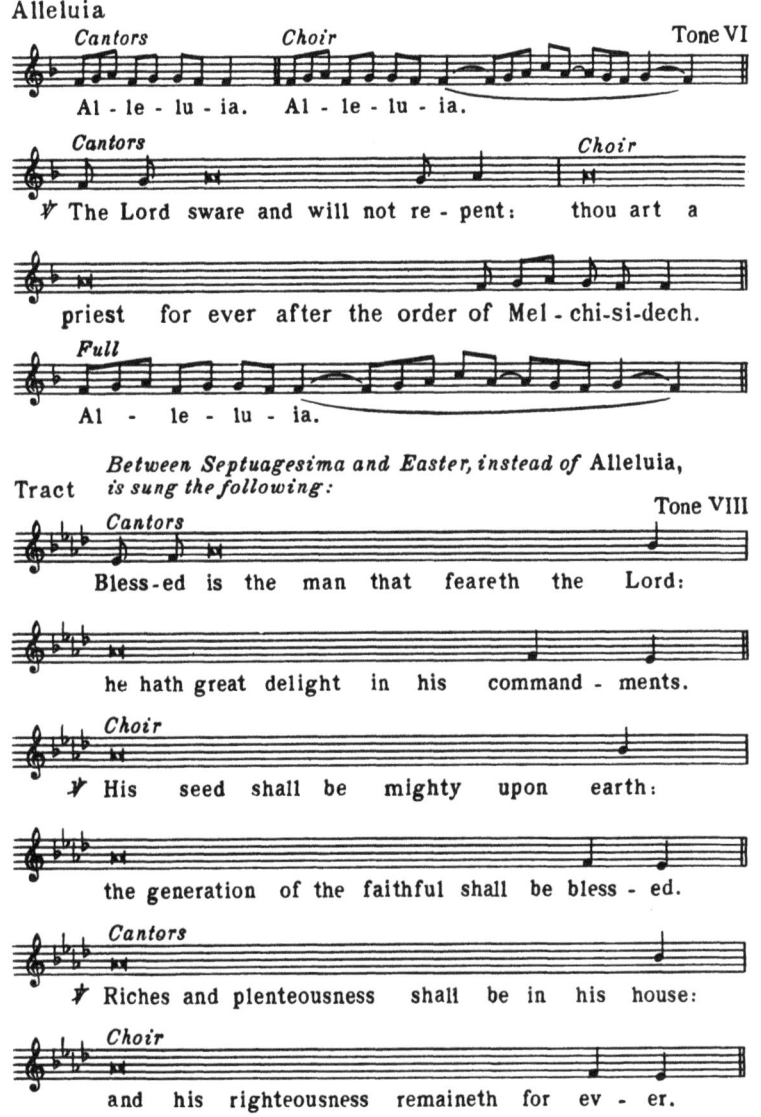

Communion Tone I

Cantors
Bless-ed is the servant whom the Lord when he com-eth shall find watch-ing:

Choir
ve - ri - ly I say unto you, he shall make him ruler o - ver all his goods.

(During Eastertide)
goods. Al - le - lu - ia.

755 THE MOST PRECIOUS BLOOD OF JESUS

Introit Tone VII

Cantors
Thou hast redeemed us O Lord, by thy blood, out of every kindred, and tongue, and peo - ple and

Choir — FINE
na - tion: and hast made us a king - dom for our God.

Cantors
My song shall be alway of the loving kind-ness of the Lord:

Choir
with my mouth will I ever be shewing thy truth from one gen-er-a-tion to an - o - ther.

Cantors Glo - ry be. *Full* Thou hast *(etc.)*

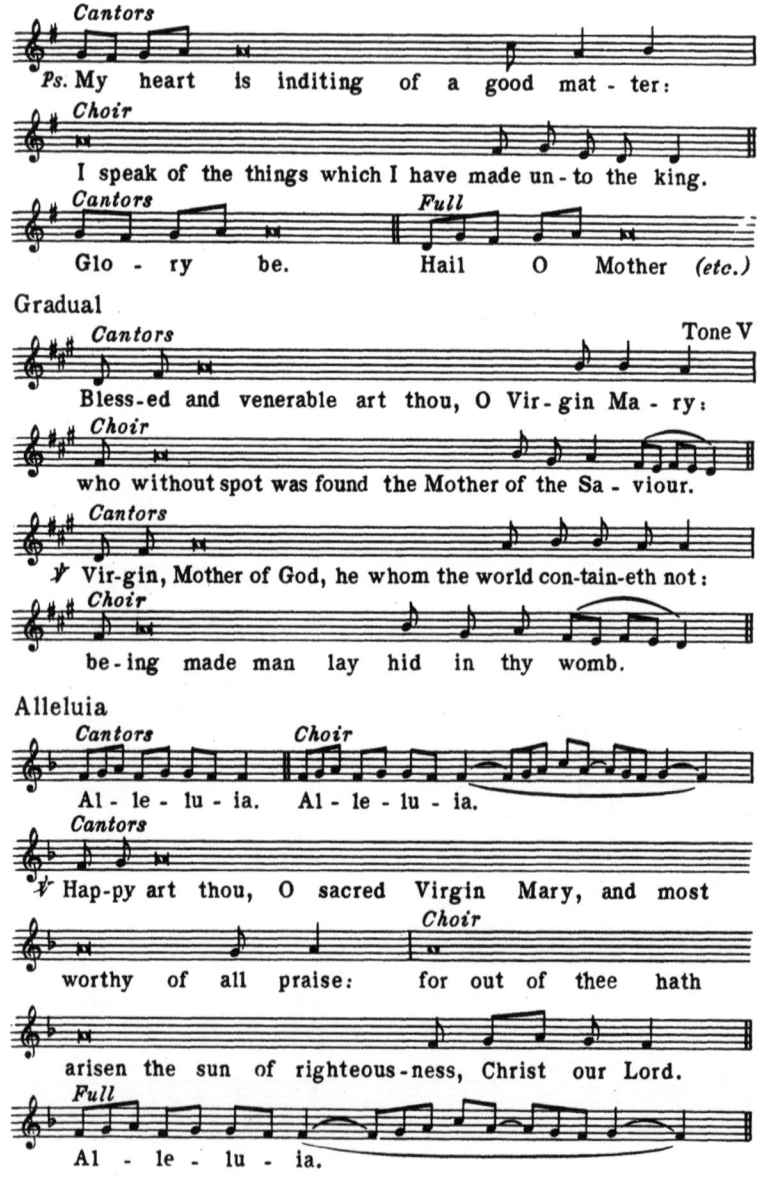

17

Offertory   Tone II

Cantors
Bless-ed art thou, O Virgin Mary, who didst bear the cre-

Choir
-a-tor of all things: thou brought-est forth him who made thee, and for ever re-main-est a Vir-gin.

Communion   Tone I

Cantors
Bless-ed is the womb of the Vir-gin Ma-ry:

Choir
that bore the Son of the ev-er last-ing Fa-ther.

In Eastertide
ever lasting Fa-ther. Al-le-lu-ia.

757 SS. JOHN FISHER AND THOMAS MORE MM.

Introit   Tone VII

Cantors
Great are the troubles of the righteous, but the Lord

Choir
delivereth them out of all: the Lord keepeth all their bones;

FINE
so that not one of them is bro-ken.

Cantors   *Choir*
Ps. I will alway give thanks un to the Lord: his praise shall ever

Cantors   *Full*
be in my mouth. Glo-ry be. Great are the *(etc.)*

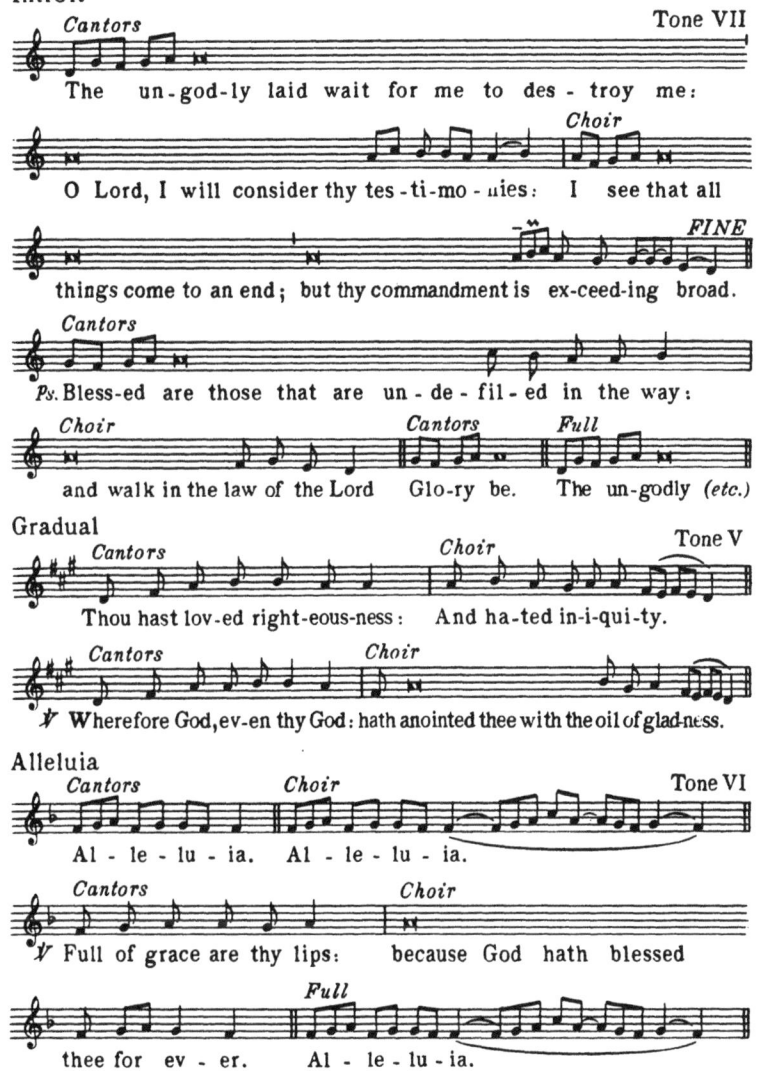

759 ST. ANNE. MOTHER OF THE B.V. MARY

Gradual, Alleluia *and* Offertory, *as for St. Mary Magdalene page 19*

Communion

Cantors — *Choir* — Tone I

Full of grace are thy lips: be-cause God hath, blessed thee for ev - er and ev - er.

760 THE TRANSFIGURATION OF OUR LORD

Introit

Cantors — *Choir* — Tone VII

The lighten-ings shone up-on the ground: the earth was mov-ed and shook with-al. *FINE* *Ps.* O how amiable are thy dwell-ings thou Lord of hosts: my soul hath a desire and longing to enter into the courts of the Lord Glo - ry be. *Full* The lighten - ings (etc.)

Gradual

Cantors — *Choir* — Tone V

Thou art fair-er than the child-ren of men: full of grace are thy lips. ℣ My heart is inditing of a good matter, I speak of the things which I have made un-to the King: *Choir* my tongue is the pen of a read-y wri - ter.

762 THE ASSUMPTION OF THE B.V. MARY

Introit — Tone VII

Cantors: There ap-peared a great wonder in heaven; a woman clo-thed with the sun: *Choir:* And the moon under her feet, and upon her head a crown of twelve stars. **FINE**

Cantors: Ps. O sing unto the Lord a new song: *Choir:* for he hath done mar-vel-lous things. *Cantors:* Glo-ry be. *Full:* There ap-peared (etc.)

Gradual — Tone V

Cantors: Heark-en O daughter, and consider, and in-cline thine ear: *Choir:* for the King delighteth greatly in thy beau-ty. *Cantors:* ℣ All glor-ious the King's daugh-ter en-ter-eth in: *Choir:* her cloth-ing is of wrought gold.

Alleluia — Tone VI

Cantors: Al-le-lu-ia. *Choir:* Al-le-lu-ia.

Cantors: ℣ Ma-ry is taken up into heav-en: *Choir:* the hosts of an-gels re-joice. *Full:* Al-le-lu-ia.

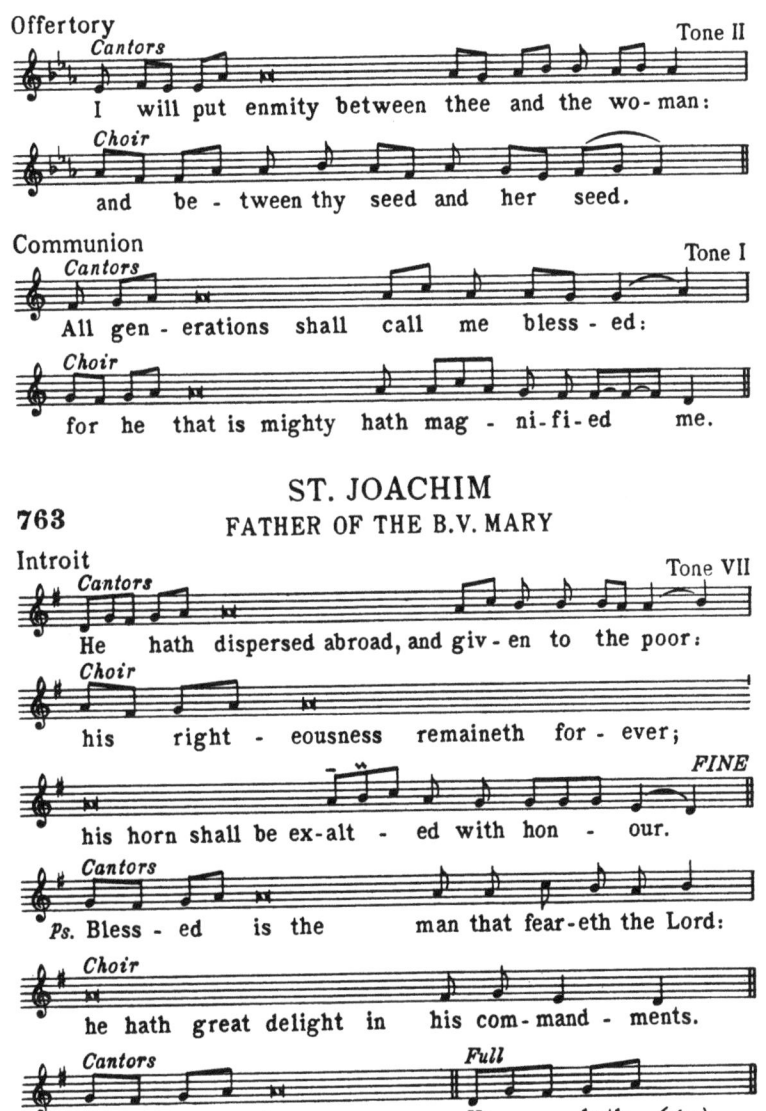

Gradual
Tone V

Cantors: He hath dispersed abroad, and given to the poor:

Choir: his righteousness remaineth for ever.

Cantors: ℣ His seed shall be mighty upon earth:

Choir: the generation of the faithful shall be blessed.

Alleluia
Tone VI

Cantors: Alleluia. **Choir:** Alleluia.

Cantors: ℣ Joachim, spouse of Saint Anne, of the gracious Virgin the father: **Choir:** here to thy servants bring safety and aid from on high. **Full:** Alleluia.

Offertory *(page 163)* "With glory and worship" in Part II
Communion *(page 167)* "A faithful and wise servant" in Part II

764 THE IMMACULATE HEART OF B.V. MARY

Introit — Tone VII

Cantors: Let us come boldly un-to the throne of grace:
Choir: that we may obtain mercy, and find grace to help in time of need. *Ps.* My heart is inditing of a good mat-ter: I speak of the things which I have made un-to the King. Glo-ry be. Let us come *(etc.)*

Gradual — Tone V

Cantors: My heart shall be joyful in Thy sal-va-tion:
Choir: I will sing of the Lord because he hath dealt so lovingly with me; yea I will praise the name of the Lord most high-est. ℣ They shall remember thy name from one generation to an-o-ther: there fore shall the people give thanks unto thee, world with-out end.

NATIVITY OF B.V.M. *Same as* Visitation, *page 15.*

765 SEVEN SORROWS OF B.V.M.

Introit — Tone VII

Cantors: There stood by the Cross of Jesus his Mother, and his Mother's sister, Mary the wife of Cleo-phas:

Choir: and Sa-lome, and Ma-ry Mag-da-le-ne. *FINE*

Cantors: ℣ Je-sus said unto his Mother, Wo-man be-hold thy Son:

Choir: Then said He to the disciple, Be-hold thy Mo-ther.

Cantors: Glo-ry be. *Full:* There stood by the Cross *(etc.)*

Gradual — Tone V

Cantors: Mourn-full and weeping art thou, O Vir-gin Ma-ry:

Choir: Standing by the Cross of the Lord Jesus, thy Son, the Re-deem-er.

Cantors: ℣ Vir-gin Mother of God, he whom the whole world containeth not, endureth this tor-ment of the Cross:

Choir: the au-thor of life made man.

THE MOST SACRED ROSARY

Introit — Tone VII

Cantors: Rejoice we all, and praise the Lord, celebrating a holy day in honour of the Virgin Mary:
Choir: in whose solemnity the Angels are joyful, and glorify the Son of God. *FINE*
Cantors: Ps. My heart is inditing of a good matter:
Choir: I speak of the things which I have made unto the King.
Cantors: Glory be.
Full: Rejoice we all (*etc.*)

Gradual — Tone V

Cantors: Because of the word of truth, of meekness and righteousness:
Choir: and thy right hand shall teach thee terrible things.
Cantors: ℣ Hearken, O daughter, and consider, incline thine ear:
Choir: so shall the King have pleasure in thy beauty.

Alleluia — Tone VI

Cantors: Alleluia. *Choir:* Alleluia.

767 MOTHERHOOD OF B.V. MARY

Introit — Tone VII

Cantors: Be-hold a virgin shall con-ceive and bear a Son:
Choir: and shall call his name, Em-man-u-el. *FINE*
Cantors: Ps. O sing un-to the Lord a new song: for he hath done mar-vel-lous things. *Choir:* Glo-ry be. *Full:* Be-hold a virgin (etc.)

Gradual — Tone V

Cantors: There shall come forth a rod out of the stem of Jes - se:
Choir: And a branch shall rise up out of his roots.
Cantors: ℣ And the spi-rit of the Lord: *Choir:* shall rest up-on him.

Alleluia — Tone VI

Cantors: Al - le - lu - ia. *Choir:* Al - le - lu - ia.
Cantors: ℣ Vir-gin, Mother of God, he whom the world con-tain-eth not:
Choir: being made man lay hid in thy womb.
Full: Al - le - lu - ia.

Offertory

Cantors — Tone II

When Mary his Mother was espoused to Joseph:

Choir

she was found with child of the Holy Ghost.

Communion

Cantors — Tone I — *Choir*

Blessed be the womb of the Virgin Mary that bare for us the Son of the eternal Father.

768 OUR LORD JESUS CHRIST THE KING

Introit

Cantors — Tone VII

Worthy is the Lamb that was slain to receive power, and riches, and wisdom, and strength, and honour:

Choir

to him be glory and dominion for ever and ever.

FINE Cantors

Ps. Give the King thy judgements,

Choir

O God: and thy righteousness unto the King's Son.

Cantors — *Full*

Glory be. Worthy is the Lamb *(etc.)*

higher than the kings of the earth. ℣ His seed also will I make to endure for ev - er: and his throne as the days of hea - ven.

During Easter-tide the Gradual *is omitted, and the foregoing* Alleluia *is sung, followed at once by:*

℣ And he hath on his vesture and on his thigh a Name writ - ten: King of kings, and Lord of lords. Al - le - lu - ia.

Offertory Tone II

De - sire of me, and I shall give thee the heathen for thine in - he - ri - tance: and the utmost parts of the earth for thy pos - ses - sion.

Communion Tone I

The Lord re - main - eth a King for ev - er: The Lord shall give his people the bless - ing of peace.

FEASTS OF THE B.V. MARY

769

Introit *Same as* Visitation, *page 15.*
Gradual *Same as* Visitation,

Alleluia

Tone VI

Cantors — Al - le - lu - ia. *Choir* — Al - le - lu - ia.

Cantors
℣ After child birth, O Virgin, Thou didst remain in-vi-o-late: *Choir* Mother of God in-ter-cede for us.

Full
Al - le - lu - ia.

In Advent, in place of the preceding verse:

Cantors
℣ Hail Ma-ry full of grace, the Lord is with thee: *Choir* blessed art thou a-mong wo-men.

Tract *After Septuagesima in place of the* Alleluia *the following.*

Tone VIII

Cantors
Re-joice, O Vir-gin Ma-ry: thou alone all heresy did slay. *Choir* ℣ Thou the Archangel Gabriel's mes-sage: *Cantors* didst be-lieve ℣ While yet a Virgin bearing God and man: thou after child-birth, Virgin, inviolate didst re-main *Choir* ℣ Mo-ther of God: in-ter-cede for us.

In Easter-tide, in place of the foregoing Gradual *is sung the following:*

Alleluia

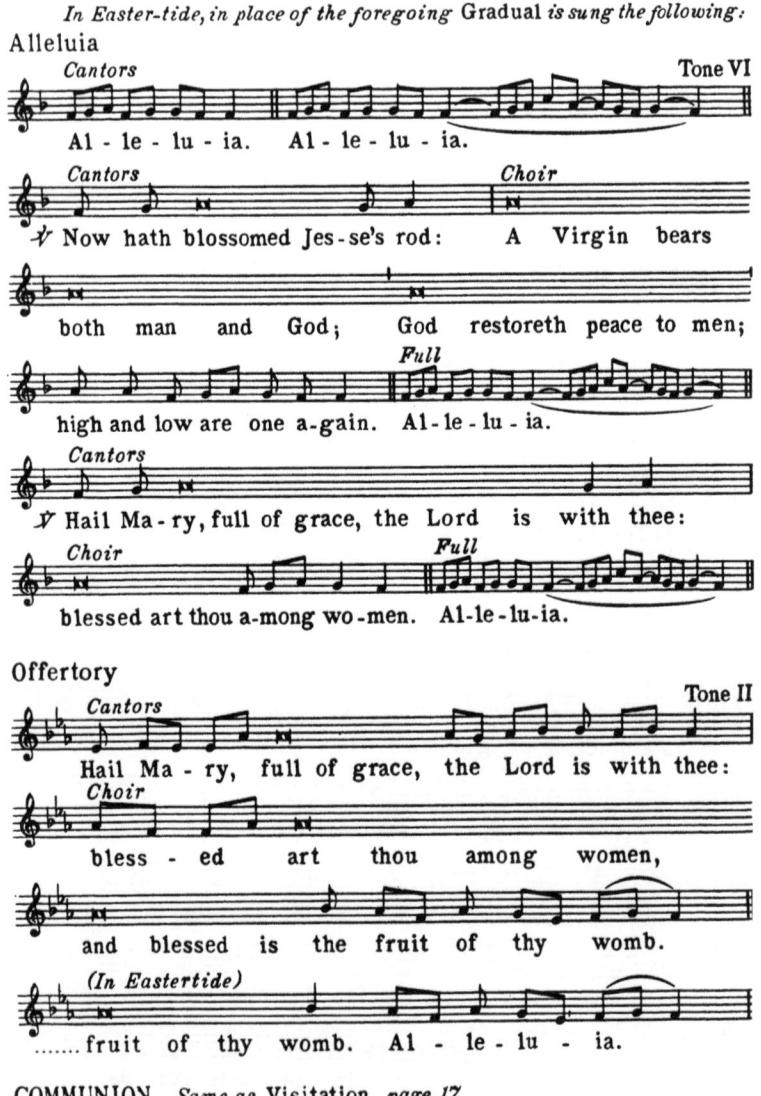

Al - le - lu - ia. Al - le - lu - ia.

℣ Now hath blossomed Jes-se's rod: A Virgin bears both man and God; God restoreth peace to men; high and low are one a-gain. Al-le-lu-ia.

℣ Hail Ma-ry, full of grace, the Lord is with thee: blessed art thou a-mong wo-men. Al-le-lu-ia.

Offertory

Hail Ma-ry, full of grace, the Lord is with thee: bless-ed art thou among women, and blessed is the fruit of thy womb.

(In Eastertide)
...... fruit of thy womb. Al - le - lu - ia.

COMMUNION *Same as* Visitation, *page 17.*

770 **HOLY SOVEREIGN PONTIFFS**

Introit — Tone VII

Cantors: If thou lovest me, Simon Peter:
Choir: feed my lambs, feed my sheep. *FINE*

(In Eastertide) Choir: feed my lambs, feed my sheep. Alleluia, Alleluia. *FINE*

Cantors: Ps. I will magnify thee, O Lord, for Thou hast set me up.
Choir: and not made my foes to triumph over me.
Cantors: Glory be. *Full:* If thou lovest (etc.)

Gradual — Tone V

Cantors: Let them exalt him in the congregation of the people:
Choir: and praise him in the seat of the elders.
Cantors: ℣ O that men would praise the Lord for his goodness
Choir: and declare the wonders that he doeth for the children of men.

INDEX

	Page
THE CONCEPTION B.V.M.	1
ST. THOMAS OF CANTERBURY	4
THE HOLY FAMILY	6
THE SOLEMNITY OF ST. JOSEPH	8
ST. AUGUSTINE OF CANTERBURY	10
THE MOST PRECIOUS BLOOD OF JESUS	13
THE VISITATION OF B.V.M.	15
SS. JOHN FISHER AND THOMAS MORE, MM.	17
ST. MARY MAGDALENE	19
ST. ANNE	20
THE TRANSFIGURATION	21
ST. LAURENCE	22
THE ASSUMPTION OF B.V.M.	24
ST. JOACHIM	25
THE IMMACULATE HEART OF B.V.M.	27
THE NATIVITY OF B.V.M.	15
THE SEVEN SORROWS OF B.V.M.	29
THE MOST SACRED ROSARY	31
THE MOTHERHOOD OF B.V.M.	33
OUR LORD JESUS CHRIST THE KING	34
FEASTS OF THE B.V.M.	37
HOLY SOVEREIGN PONTIFFS	39

www.ingramcontent.com/pod-product-compliance
Ingram Content Group UK Ltd.
Pitfield, Milton Keynes, MK11 3LW, UK
UKHW041413180426
11947UKWH00007B/111